Teaching and Learning

Key Stage 2

Differentiated Answ

Contents

Literacy

Year 6

Introduction

This Year 6 Literacy Differentiation Answer Book contains answers to all of the questions in each unit of the Year 6 Activity Book, providing a quick and easy comprehensive reference for teachers.

Some of the activities encourage a variety of responses, in which case a small selection of possible answers has been provided as a guide.

Letts Educational
First published 1999

Letts Educational,
Schools and Colleges Division
9-15 Aldine Street
London W12 8AW
Tel: 0181 740 2270
Fax: 0181 740 2280

Designed by Ken Vail Graphic Design,
Cambridge

British Library Cataloguing-in-Publication Data
A CIP record is available from the British Library

ISBN 1-84085-265-8

Printed in Great Britain by Ashford Colour Press

Verbs and tenses

Check it out

1.

Present tense	*Past*
At this moment I get	Yesterday I got
At this moment I do	Yesterday I did
At this moment I catch	Yesterday I caught
At this moment I stop	Yesterday I stopped
At this moment I try	Yesterday I tried
At this moment I tell	Yesterday I told
At this moment I jump	Yesterday I jumped

Practice

1.

a) I believe that smoking is bad for you. (present)
b) My mum went to the shops and bought me some chocolate. (past)
c) It will rain over most of the northwest hills tomorrow. (future)
d) The scene of this story is France and it is very exciting. (present)
e) Scientists say that people will walk on Mars within the next hundred years. (future)
f) The motorcycle was first built in England in about 1886. (past)
g) Some old people dozed in their rocking chairs on the porch. (past)
h) You will never pass your exams until you learn to work harder. (future)
I) Flowers with strong scents encourage bees to live in your garden. (present)
J) Farjad swam and swam but he could not reach the dog in time. (past)

Challenger

1.

Verb	*Yesterday I …*	*I have …*
to swim	swam	swum
to write	wrote	written
to begin	began	begun
to buy	bought	bought
to choose	chose	chosen
to come	came	come
to drink	drank	drunk
to eat	ate	eaten
to fall	fell	fallen
to forget	forgot	forgotten

Children should add two more irregular verbs to the table – these will vary

Unit 2 Active verbs

Check it out

1.

a) The wind blew strongly all night.
b) His appearance took me by surprise.
c) Suddenly, the door flew open.
d) My uncle grew the prize-winning tomatoes at the Show.
e) I told the gardener to cut the grass shorter this year.
f) The park warden hired extra staff to pick up the extra litter.
g) Gusts of wind made the candle-flame flicker mysteriously.
h) Shoppers crowded the streets in their rush to buy Christmas gifts.

Practice

1.

a) My luggage is inspected by the Customs Department./The Customs Department inspect my luggage.
b) The garage doors are operated by two guards./Two guards operate the garage doors.
c) I was guided to my seat by a young lady./A young lady guided me to my seat.
d) In our school nursery, children are looked after by Mrs Randall./Mrs Randall looks after the children in our school nursery.
e) The glass was dropped by Robert./Robert dropped the glass.
f) The mouse was chased by the cat./The cat chased the mouse.
g) All the keys had been taken by someone./Someone took all the keys.

Practice

h) The ball was kicked into the air by the girl./The girl kicked the ball into the air.

Challenger

1.

The teacher took the test tube and placed it in the flame. It was then heated until some bubbles were seen in the water. Miss Sunhilla told us to keep out of the way as it might be dangerous. The teacher took the temperature of the liquid and recorded it in the table. Then the liquid was left in a cold place in the classroom until it changed colour. While this was happening, the teacher heated the white solid in another part of the room When we saw it change colour and give off a gas, the teacher mixed them together. Finally, she washed out the test tube and returned it carefully to the shelf. By the time this had happened, we could see small blue crystals forming. The teacher/Miss Sunhilla asked us to watch them until they grew to a large size. When the experiment was complete she let us hang the pretty crystals in the class.

(Answers to the above may vary but only active verbs should be used.)

Unit 3 Passive verbs

Check it out

1.

a) The plate was dropped by my brother.
b) The robber was taken by surprise when I fought back.
c) All the sweets were eaten by the children.
d) The assembly was finished with a prayer.
e) Our summer disco was organised by the teachers.
f) An exhibition of work was put on by Class 6.
g) Several books were thrown out of the bus by the naughty girls.
h) Three pieces of jewellery are being examined by the police for fingerprints.

Practice

1.

a) Thick wool carpets deadened the noise in the hall./The noise in the hall was deadened by the thick wool carpets.
b) Radios direct the police to the crime./The police are directed to the crime by radios.
c) In the store, glass lifts take customers to the top floor./In the store, customers are taken to the top floor by glass lifts.
d) Our workshops carry out all kinds of car repairs./All kinds of car repairs are carried out by our workshops.

Practice

e) Bad storms delayed the arrival of Concorde./The arrival of Concorde was delayed by bad storms.
f) Large windows allow maximum light into the temple./Maximum light is allowed into the temple through large windows.
g) We chose a large green plant for the experiment./A large green plant was chosen for the experiment by us.
h) The dogs chased the rabbits across the field./The rabbits were chased across the field by the dogs.

Challenger

1.

a) Four children ran into the hallway and disappeared out of the door.
b) The teacher understood the children's panic.
c) My friend put his books down quietly and someone asked him to find the Headteacher.
d) The class sat patiently while he searched for the Headteacher.
e) The children obeyed the teacher and everything was fine when the four worried classmates came back in crying.
f) Someone brought some tissues in and they apologised at the end of the day.

(Answers to the above may vary but all the passive verbs should be changed into active verbs.)

Unit 4 Connectives 1

Check it out

1.

a) They could go to the theme park <u>or</u> to the circus.
b) We will not arrive until after dinner, <u>in other words</u>, we will be late.
c) Sarah can come to stay <u>but</u> she will have to sleep in the spare room.
d) I would like the soup to start <u>and</u> the steak as my next course.
e) The clown spun around in circles, <u>finally</u> ending the show with a bow.
f) Let's not have a drink here <u>because</u> it's too crowded.
g) Jemila was complaining about the food <u>until</u> the manager came.
h) We drove to visit John <u>before</u> we had lunch.
i) I was just reading my book <u>when</u> there was a knock on the door.

Practice

1.

Answers will vary, but sentences should be joined with and, but or so.

2.

Answers will vary, but sentences should be joined with when, before, although or so that.

Challenger

1. *Answers will vary but should include a connective.*

Unit 5

Connectives 2

Check it out

1.

a) The cat sat down and stretched in the sun.
b) All the birds were in the tree but they were quiet.
c) The birds all flew off, consequently the cat had no reason to be there.
d) She felt angry and flung the toy mouse into the air.
e) Tibbles walked away, firstly looking both ways for enemies.
f) Her garden was empty, but she was still on guard.
g) She was not really hungry, nevertheless she took a few mouthfuls of food.
h) I felt sorry for her although the birds had escaped.

Practice

1. *Answers will vary but new nursery rhymes must contain a connective.*

Challenger

1.

Location	*Order*	*Time*	*Argument*	*Explanation*
under	first	then	therefore	because
on	next	just then		as you can see
beside	after that		nevertheless	
	finally	until	or	in other words
		suddenly		consequently
			but	
			although	

Answers will vary to second part of **1** *but sentences must contain one word from each section of the table.*

Simple/complex sentences

Check it out

1.

a) My books <u>are</u> in the desk. (S)
b) She <u>took</u> my books as soon as the teacher looked away. (C)
c) Water <u>leaks</u> out. (S)
d) The rain <u>dripped</u> slowly from the broken drainpipe. (C)
e) Our snowman <u>melted</u> yesterday. (S)
f) All the snow <u>melted</u> because the air temperature rose in the country. (C)
g) I <u>visited</u> Paris. (S)
h) We <u>visited</u> France where I saw many fascinating castles. (C)
i) All the dogs in the kennels <u>barked</u> loudly. (C)

Practice

1.

I shall not go to Turkey although I may visit Greece.

He loves rock music because he plays guitar in a band.

It will be a disaster unless I can phone him first.

His sister fainted when she heard she had won the lottery.

We called off the football match so we returned the tickets.

There is a big stain on the ceiling where the water came in.

Mark will not give in until he finds out who stole the bike.

Practice

Stop all that noise before I get very cross.

You will go to your room unless you tell me who broke the window.

It does not matter to me whether or not you go to the concert.

Challenger

1. *Answers will vary but must contain* a subordinate clause.

Unit 7 Semi-colons and colons

Check it out

1.

a) It was spring; the daffodils appeared almost overnight.
b) I stood quietly on the platform; soon the train would arrive.
c) Judy had not done her maths homework; she would be in trouble.
d) Sue and Maureen chatted all afternoon; they have not seen each other for years.
e) Bring me a large chocolate biscuit made from brown flour; two sticky buns, but only the round ones with cherries on the top; a large portion of steamed pudding with currants and covered in custard.

2.

a) You will need the following: two eggs, one kilo of flour and some milk.
b) There was only one judgement possible: death.
c) Please note the rule: no food allowed in the computer room.
d) The referee shouted "Get off the pitch!"

Practice

1.

a) It looked as if he had no other choice; he would have to tell the truth.
b) The large wall was covered with pictures; the smaller wall had nothing on it.
c) Suddenly Tricia screamed: "It's a dirty great rat!" she said.

Practice

d) Elizabeth slept soundly on the bench; the train passed by.
e) Take note of the school's new address: 99 Arcade Street.
f) At the supermarket buy: some tins of peas, but only if they are not processed; some frozen chocolate cake, but look at the sell-by date and a litre of milk.
g) Please don't forget to bring these for the ski trip: your passport, a woolly hat and a pair of warm gloves.
h) "I'll search the bedrooms; you search the play area.
i) In the back room the cats were asleep; in the kitchen the mice ate the cheese.

Challenger

1. *Answers will vary but the advertisements should be rewritten inserting semi-colons and colons.*

Unit 8 Dashes and brackets

Check it out

1.

a) We have no room left in the hotel – let me repeat: no room.
b) Mark's mum – the famous actress, as I found out later – was on TV.
c) She wants to buy him a new suit – I can understand why.
d) There is only one instrument worth learning – the guitar.
e) He did not take account of the most important person – his guard.

2.

a) He swam across the river (as the picture showed).
b) You must give me your homework on Wednesday. (Any homework after that will not be marked.)
c) Switch on the video recorder (see Starting Instructions on page 5).

Practice

1. *Answers will vary as dashes and brackets are interchangeable.*

Challenger

More and more people - young and old - are taking up sailing. Look at the latest figures (page 20 of the magazine) which prove this. Good sailing - and of course safe sailing - is the most important thing to learn. If you are unsure of this look back at the news reports about sinking boats.

A great deal of sports (sailing, rugby, soccer) is dangerous when not played well. The most important thing to learn are the rules - and there are plenty - in order to be safe. The law makes insurance necessary before you sail but (often a fatal omission) it does not cover all dangers.

(Answers to the above may vary.)

Unit 9 Standard English

Check it out

1.

a) There were two clocks on the station wall.
b) "Look. Here is the newspaper you lost yesterday," I replied.
c) My grandma gave me a new computer for Christmas.
d) All my toys have my name written on them in case they are stolen.
e) Each of the actors was given an extra clap at the end of the show.
f) No, Mike isn't allowed to go to the cinema this evening.
g) Does anybody want to go to the pantomime this year?
h) My mum doesn't allow us to go to concerts by ourselves.

Practice

1.

a) The two boys were fighting in the street.
b) Each of the sweets in the packet was wrapped in coloured foil.
c) "I haven't done anything," my brother shouted.
d) We did the washing up after Christmas dinner.
e) My mum said she didn't want anything for her birthday.
f) The policewoman gave me a warning when she caught me in the orchard.
g) Neither Fred nor his brother was allowed out to play.
h) Louis hadn't been anywhere near the window when it smashed.

Challenger

1.

"Who's got my sweets? I haven't got any left. I spent a pound on them yesterday. I bet that Ray is eating them."

"There's no point blaming me. The sweets were in my locker. John and I were going to eat them tomorrow. I bet that man over there has got them."

"No. He doesn't know anything. I've already asked him. He gave his sweets away to someone else. Those children aren't coming today. That means we haven't got any food today."

"Wait a minute. Look in that cupboard on your left. I think that's the food that I bought the other day. Does anyone know if it belongs to anyone? I don't want any trouble if we eat it."

"No problem. All the adults have gone to work. Great … this food is delicious."

Unit 10 Parts of speech

Check it out

1.

a) The <u>cat</u> sat quietly on the mat. (noun)
b) We jumped over the wall and <u>fell</u> into the mud. (verb)
c) The boy loved the chocolate in the box, but he did not allow <u>her</u> any. (pronoun)
d) As a Christmas present, he bought me a <u>beautiful</u> gold vase. (adjective)
e) Dickens wrote his novels <u>quickly</u> so they could be published in parts. (adverb)

2. *Answers will vary but should include:*

a) adjective
b) verb
c) noun
d) noun or adverb
e) conjunction
f) pronoun

Practice

1. *Answers will vary but must include* nouns, verbs, conjunctions, pronouns *and* adverbs.

2. *Answers will vary*

Challenger

1. *Answers will vary*

nit 1 Changing active to passive

Check it out

.
a) The cats killed the mice.
b) The mice were (hunted) by the cats.
c) I have decided upon a daring plan.
d) A plan has finally been (decided) upon.
e) We received your order in the post yesterday.
f) People always find mushrooms in that field.
g) Our leader was injured in a car crash.
h) We all ran over to see the accident.

Practice

1.
a) An old and historic parliament rules our country.
b) Members of the public over 18 vote for members of Parliament.
c) The House of Lords takes some votes.
d) The House of Commons decides most of the laws.
e) Parliament makes the laws of our country.
f) The government ensures law and order in our country.
g) Parliament invites the Queen to visit every year.

2. *Answers will vary but the passage should be rewritten changing all the active verbs to the passive form.*

Challenger

1.
The flight was delayed by bad weather so we had hours to spend at the airport. We stood on the roof. The planes were directed in and out by radar. The noise was deadened by earplugs. Frightening noises were still heard by us. A girl was in trouble. The police were directed by shouts to the girl. A man was chased around the airport by their dog. The delay worried us. Our trip had been organised for us by my sister for her wedding. A message was sent to my sister. A phone was found by my friend. The money was put into the machine by him. Nothing happened and the money was lost. The wait was miserable. A bottle was smashed in the distance. The room was cleaned by a lady.

Changing passive to active

Check it out

1.

Active verbs	*Passive verbs*
sat	wounded
were	taken
took	
looked	
kept, gave	

Practice

1.

Trout are found in this stream. People find trout in this stream.

The new submarine was launched by the Queen last week. The Queen launched the new submarine last week.

My sister is looked after by Aunt Sophie. Aunt Sophie looks after my sister.

Our car was parked by students. Students parked our car.

The new printer is powered by microwaves. Microwaves power the new printer.

My bag was examined by the police. The police examined my bag.

Children should add two more examples underlining the subject of each sentence and circling each verb.

2.

A sentence is in the active form when the subject of the verb is actually performing the action of the sentence. When the action of the verb is being done to the subject by someone or something else it is passive.

Challenger

1.

Sarah made a scream. Immediately the villains seized four guards and dragged them to the Master's feet. Someone tied up John. Superman saw the guards' attack. He stuck his foot out and caught one villain in mid air. He pinned him to the wall. The creature begged for mercy. Superman looked at Sarah. Should the villain be released or sent to prison?

nit 13 Formal language

Check it out

1.

orename	– Your first name.
Marital status	– If you are married or single.
Duplicate	– A copy of something.
Maiden name	– A woman's name before marriage.
Block letters	– Capital letters.
On the reverse	– On the back of something.
Nationality	– The country you come from.
Occupation	– The work that you do.

Practice

1.

Formal words	*Informal words*
beverages	drinks
consume	eat
distinguishing marks	scars
conceal	hide
reside	live
dwelling	house
superior	boss
request	ask
endorse	sign
reverse	the back
remuneration	pay

Challenger

1. *Answers will vary but possible examples are:*

a) Office
b) Laboratory
c) Park
d) Park
e) Office
f) Supermarket or other car park
g) Mail order company
h) Any public service
i) Pub/bar etc.

Unit 14 Revision of clauses

Check it out

1.

a) Because I (loved) it.
b) If you (press) that button.
c) She (stayed) in the garden.
d) He could (reach) the books.
e) When it (stops) raining.
f) Her coat was (torn).
g) Although it (is) green.
h) So he will (win).

Practice

1.

a) The car broke down in the rain but it started again when it dried out.
b) The crow flew away when the hunter with a gun arrived.
c) My dad drove all night although he was too tired to drive.
d) My nose was bright red because it was freezing cold outside.
e) We drank warm cocoa after we finished building the bonfire.
f) I was allowed to open my presents when my father arrived at the party.
g) A policeman must wear a uniform when he gives evidence in court.
h) I am writing my story so/because I can get it published.
i) The Queen was arriving so the security was important.

Challenger

1. *Answers will vary but must have a new clause added to:*

a) I will not go to the concert because …
b) She left the classroom party before …
c) The roof will not be mended unless …
d) You will not find the map until …
e) It was a sunny day so …
f) Sheila could not make out whether …
g) The wicked stepmother disappeared when …
h) The police inspector could not think how …

Complex sentences 1

Check it out

1.

a) He scored the goal when the keeper was injured on the ground.
b) The red car shot around the corner and crashed into the tree.
c) John's jacket was cheap but looked expensive.
d) I will not go out tonight because I have a headache.
e) Because I do not like her, I will not share my lunch.
f) If I go to the film, I will sit by myself.

Practice

1.

a) Charlie Chaplin was a famous comedian who died a while ago.
b) The Italian, who used to play for an English team, now manages a French team.
c) Robin Hood, who lived in Nottingham, robbed the rich to give to the poor.
d) My mum, who is a great mechanic, owns the garage around the corner.
e) John Lennon was a member of the Beatles who died in New York.

2.

a) The table, which is an antique, is two hundred years old.
b) The football match, which was between two London teams, ended after the first goal.
c) Fresh strawberries, which are good for the skin, are not always available.

Practice

d) The Rocky mountains, which are parallel to the coast, get most of the rain.
e) The Police force, which was founded by Robert Peel, celebrated its anniversary recently.

Challenger

1.

a) No one will leave the class until the Headteacher has made her choice.
b) You need to learn to swim so you can perform lifesaving.
c) His father bought him a new computer but he should have waited for the sales.
d) My cousin was very confident but he did not pass the exam.
e) Drive for an hour until you pass an old church with a steeple.

(Note answers to the above may vary – these are sample suggestions)

Complex sentences 2

Check it out

1.

a) The video was so dull that I fell asleep.

b) The market stall was not making them enough money so they sold it.

c) When I am seventeen, I am allowed to get a driving licence.

d) Until I check with my mum, I can't tell you if I can go out tomorrow.

e) Get that mess cleaned up in the kitchen before I tell your mother!

f) You will never find the secret plans unless you look in the right place.

g) While the police looked through the house, I searched the bin.

Practice

1.

a) Athens, the capital of Greece, is famous for the Parthenon.

b) Manchester, a city in the north, has excellent road communications.

c) Roald Dahl, the author of many children's books, died a few years ago.

d) Tennis, a popular summer sport, is played outside from May to September.

e) Silk, made from the pupa of silkworms, makes fine material.

f) Albert Einstein, a famous mathematician, discovered many things.

g) French, taught to many children in schools, is a useful European language.

h) Diwali, the festival of lights, is an important Hindu celebration.

Challenger

1. *Answers will vary but must be one sentence incorporating* connectives *and* commas.

Unit 17 Conditionals 1

Check it out

1.

a) I <u>should be</u> grateful if you would send me some information.
b) I <u>could not</u> eat the chocolate as it was bitter.
c) I told you that you <u>would be</u> sorry.
d) If I <u>could do</u> tapestry like that, I would be proud.
e) If you are tired, you <u>should go</u> to bed.
f) We <u>would not</u> let him out until he gave us back the bag.
g) <u>Could I</u> borrow that video if I promise to return it tomorrow?
h) She <u>would have</u> passed her exams if she had done more work.
i) If the weather is fine, we <u>should be</u> able to go on a picnic.

Practice

1.

If I water the garden – the grass will grow.

If I had watered the garden – the grass would have grown.

If I had taken the money – I would have been rich.

If I take the money – I will be rich.

If she pulls my hair again – I will scream and shout.

If she had pulled my hair again – I would have screamed and shouted.

Practice

2. The conditional sentences contain verbs that tell you that the action might happen because it depends on something or somebody else.

Challenger

1. *Answers will vary but children should complete the conditional sentences with suitable endings:*

a) I should …
b) If I had …
c) Could you …
d) Would you …
e) The cat could …
f) When she had …

2. *Answers will vary but children should write five conditional sentences of their own and explain what makes conditional sentences different from other verb tenses.*

Unit 18 Conditionals 2

Check it out

1.

a) She will be going to the ball if the Fairy Godmother arrives. (F)
b) If I don't work harder, I will have to leave school. (F)
c) If I had passed my driving test the first time, I would not be so desperate. (P)
d) Whether she found it or not, she would have to tell her father. (F)
e) You will not find a better holiday in the world than here. (F)
f) If you had got up earlier you would have seen the sunset. (P)
g) We will have to tell him tonight before the post arrives tomorrow. (F)
h) No one would notice if you left the party early. (F)

Practice

1. *Answers will vary but must include a total of 24 conditional sentences starting with* If (present tense), If (past tense), If … had … (past tense), I will, I would, I would have *(4 of each)*

Challenger

1.

a) My mum could be given help in the house./My mum should be given help in the house.
b) Trevor should pass his driving test in my car./Trevor passed his driving test in my car.
c) I would give them all my money for charity./I should give them all my money for charity.

2. *Answers will vary but children should explain how the meanings of these groups of sentences are different because of the different tenses of the verbs used.*

Unit 19 Shortening sentences 1

Check it out

1.

pto – please turn over

kph – kilometres per hour

Rd – Road

anon – anonymous

Ave – Avenue

2.

USA, BC, Sq, RSPCA, PO

Practice

1.

a) aquarium
b) dock
c) stables
d) theatre

2.

a) extinguisher
b) erase
c) emigrate
d) hospital

3.

b) media
c) household furniture
d) occupations

Challenger

1.

a) The car stopped working because it ran out of petrol.
b) We shall visit the zoo as soon as possible.
c) The workers squeezed the grapes to get the wine.
d) The water drains away through the hole in the bucket.
e) The fisherman lifted the fish clear out of the water.
f) The remark was typical of my sister.
g) My mother is in hospital to have an operation.
h) Our house is made of wood because it is cheap.

Shortening sentences 2

Check it out

1.

a) Our cat chased the mouse into its hole.
b) My uncle from Italy sat down and ordered a drink.
c) The girl from next door loved diving into the pool.
d) The clown fell from the horse into the sand of the arena.
e) My cousin read her new book.
f) Our guest at the hotel phoned the police.
g) Jim signed my autograph book.

Practice

1.

a) Two men killed when car hit lorry.
b) Staff meeting started at three o'clock.
c) Egyptians covered bodies in bandages.
d) Oscar awarded to unknown, Sarah Biggs.
e) Our new car was large and red.
f) Outnumbered by pirates they wouldn't give up.
g) Important things rescued from flood waters.

(Answers to the above may vary.)

Challenger

1. Pat had to collect sister from nursery, buy some milk, pay electricity bill and clean the car.

nit
:1

Reports

Check it out

.

ı) In Britain there are fourteen species of bat. These bats live in the south and west of England. There are very few bats in Scotland. All the bats are small. On average they weigh 4g and have a wing span of 20cm. There are a few myths about bats. 'As blind as a bat' is completely wrong. Bats can see but not in colour. Bats are under threat now more than most other wildlife.

ɔ) The verbs are in the present tense.

c) Number of species = 14
Weight = 4g
Wing span = 20cm

d) The writer talks about them generally using pronouns these, they.

e) Yes – general introduction, details, conclusion.

f) *Answers will vary.*

Practice

.

1etals are an essential part of our lives. 1ost of the metals we use began their ives in the earth. An ore is a mixture of netal and other rock. When we make ılloys we make it like toffee. We place ıll the ingredients in a pan and heat it. The ore turns to liquid and is poured ɔff. The process of extracting the metal rom the ore is called smelting.

Challenger

1. *Answers will vary but should follow the plan.*

Unit 22 Recounts

Check it out

1.

a) Tracy went to nursery every day. She learnt how to write.
b) I began school in the autumn and left the following term.
c) Mike swam the river every year and climbed exhausted on the bank.
d) My mum forgot the sweets and gave me an apple.
e) Jim wrote the cheque and gave it to him.
f) I forgot my lunch so I ate a chocolate bar.

2.

You need an electric toaster.

First, cut some bread.

Then select the cooking time on the dial of the toaster.

Insert the bread.

When the toast pops up, remove it and butter it.

Finally, eat it!

Practice

1.

The bank in the High Street was full of bored people. Robert **and** (I) stood in a queue **and** watched impatiently **when, suddenly,** (we) saw the man in black suddenly barge through the doors.

"**What** shall we do?" (I) whispered.

Before Robert could reply, the alarm rang. **Next**, the thief looked around (him), threw down the bag and ran.

This was a frightening experience **and** (I) would not like to live through it again.

a) Pronouns circled as above.
b) Verbs underlined as above. The past tense is used.
c) The information is about a bank raid. It has a beginning, a middle and an end.
d) He sets the scene by describing the bored people in the bank and the queues.
e) Robert, the person giving the account and the 'man in black'. Only Robert is named.
f) Connectives and words which start sentences shown in bold type (as above).

Challenger

1. *Answers will vary but should incorporate the listed features.*

Unit 23 Instructions

Check it out

.

ı) Switch off the computer.
›) Pull the joystick.
:) Eat another biscuit.
ꟷ) Write out the spellings.
ɜ) Sit down and be quiet.

.

eave the house. First turn right then ʋalk for ten minutes. Next turn left and top at the bus stop. Then cross the oad. After that walk up the side street nd enter the market.

Note answers to the above will vary – ample suggestion)

Practice

.

ainting a wall

ou need: a large paint brush, mulsion paint, protective clothing, overings to protect furnishing.

rocedure: Paint large areas a little at time. Paint vertical stripes first, then nake cross-strokes to join them. Do ot put any more paint on your brush. ontinue to smooth gently – back into ne painted area. Limit yourself to a nall area so the paint does not dry oo quickly.

) Verbs underlined as above. They use the command form.
) The writing is more like a list.

Practice

c) A list of equipment is important because without the equipment you could not carry out the instructions. Equipment should written at the beginning.
e) Instructions should be written in the correct order because otherwise people may end up with the wrong end result.
f) Answers will vary

Challenger

1. *Answers will vary but children should write a set of instructions choosing a subject from those listed.*

Unit 24 Promotion

Check it out

1.

Answers will vary but suggested examples are:

a) Art-related products/paint etc.
b) Cleaning materials.
c) Chocolate product.
d) Fish and chip shop.
e) Tea/teashop.
f) Hairdressers.
g) Garage/tyres etc.

Practice

1.

strong – stronger – strongest

lucky – luckier – luckiest

thin – thinner – thinnest

good – better – best

beautiful – more beautiful – most beautiful

lovely – lovelier – loveliest

handsome – more handsome/handsomer – most handsome/handsomest

2. *Answers will vary but children should find as many synonyms as possible for* good *and* big.

3. *Answers will vary but children should rewrite the advert to make it more interesting.*

Challenger

1. *Answers will vary but children should write an advertisement for TV, cinema or radio.*

Unit 25 Explanations

Check it out

1.

Locks <u>are built</u> to control the flow of rivers. They <u>let</u> boats move up- or down-stream, but <u>prevent</u> water from being <u>wasted</u>. Locks <u>are</u> small and <u>are</u> usually <u>made</u> of two gates which <u>are</u> closed to <u>let</u> water <u>escape</u> or to <u>pump</u> it in. This <u>is</u> how boats <u>can</u> <u>travel</u> upstream. A series of locks <u>is</u> like a flight of stairs.

a) Verbs are underlined as above. They are in the present tense.
b) Locks are built to control the flow of rivers.
c) Why we have locks – what they do – what they look like – how they operate.
d) *Answers will vary (e.g.* lock gates)
e) *Answers will vary*
f) There is nothing personal in this explanation so personal writing would not be an appropriate style.

Practice

1.

The master was pulled up the road by his dog. He was met by his uncle and they shared a joke. The teacher told him off for being late when he arrived at school.

2. *Answers will vary but should use connectives.*

3. *Answers will vary but should include connectives to do with cause and effect.*

Challenger

1. *Answers will vary but should include the listed steps.*

Unit 26 Persuasion

Check it out

1.

Foxhunting is cruel and I believe it should be banned. Every thinking person in this country knows they are hunted just for fun. To prove this, I talked to a shepherd last week who saw one defencelessly killed. Did you know the fox was really helping the country and is not a nuisance at all? In fact, it helps to keep down harmful pests.

a) Opening statement underlined as above.
b) It is a personal statement. "I believe" tells you this.
c) The writer uses two different arguments.
d) Verbs underlined as above (first statement in bold) . Past and present tense has been used.
e) I believe, to prove this, in fact, did you know

Practice

1.

a) Cats are a nuisance. They continually dig up my flowerbeds and scratch my lawn. They need to be kept in by their owners. If I see one in my garden I will chase it away.
b) *Answers will vary but must be in the* present tense.

2. *Answers will vary*

Challenger

1. *Answers will vary but should follow the plan provided.*

Unit 27 Discussion

Check it out

1.

In Britain, road accidents to <u>do</u> with drink-driving <u>are</u> the commonest cause of death in young people. I <u>believe</u> that people who <u>drink</u> and <u>drive</u> <u>are</u> not only <u>being</u> stupid with their own lives but <u>are</u> also selfish because they <u>endanger</u> the lives of others. People <u>can</u> be crippled for life through no fault of their own.

a) Verbs are underlined as above. They are in the present tense.

b) First statement has been emboldened (to avoid confusion with underlined verbs). The opening sentence introduces the discussion by stating a factual piece of information and relating drink-driving to the cause of death in young people.

c) *Answers will vary*

2. *Answers will vary but should include a suitable ending to these sentences:*

a) Young drivers cause most accidents, because …

b) They often drive faster, therefore …

c) Many people think they should not drive alone, however …

Practice

1.

a) Doctor Smith said that a person who smoked every day was endangering their health.

b) Jim said that he didn't like being in a room full of smokers because it made his clothes smell.

c) Nita said there was nothing wrong with smoking and she should be allowed to do what she likes.

d) My teacher said that if she caught any of us smoking she would be very disappointed.

2.

a) Mum said that it didn't make you look any more important.

b) Reena said that Ranjit wanted to look cool.

c) Jimmy boasted that he smoked all the time with his friends.

d) Chris replied that he thought he was wasting his time and money.

Challenger

1. *Answers will vary but should follow the stated plan*

Formal styles of writing

Check it out

1.

Formal style of letter	*Informal style of letter*
Dear Sir or Madam	Dear Mum
Yours faithfully	Cheers Jim
I hope this finds you in the best of health	How are you?
Yours sincerely	Best wishes
I refer to your letter of last month	love and kisses

2. *Answers will vary*

Practice

1.

a) For your safety you must comply with all the signs.
b) Emergency exit: cabin door operation.
c) Seats 6A and 6B are designated as emergency seats only.
d) If you meet these criteria, please identify the exit nearest to you.
e) Review the information on the back of this card.
f) Keep your belt fastened unless crew assistance is required.
g) Infant flotation devices are available.
h) Identify yourself to a crewmember to be re-seated.
i) To sit in the exit seat you must be independent of responsibilities for another person.

Practice

2.

a) For your safety you must follow all the signs.
b) Emergency exit: cabin door operation.
c) Seats 6A and 6B are to be used as emergency seats only.
d) If you meet these qualities, please look for the exit nearest to you.
e) Read the information on the back of this card.
f) Keep your belt fastened unless crew e is required.
g) Infant lifejackets are available.
h) Make yourself known to a crewmember to be re-seated.
i) To sit in the exit seat you must be alone.

(Note answers to the above will vary – sample suggestions only)

Challenger

1. *Answers will vary but should use less formal language*

ìit 9 Language investigation 1

Check it out

.
Vhistle and flute – A suit
ıpples and pears – The stairs
rouble and strife – The wife
arnet fair – Hair
lates of meat – Feet
oaf of bread – My head
lorth and south – Your mouth
ees and honey – Money

Practice

.

ımerican word or expression	*What we would use*	*American word or expression*	*What we would use*
Clothes pins	Clothes pegs	Chips	Crisps
An elevator	A lift	An apartment	A flat
Vest	T-shirt	Checkers	Draughts
Sidewalk	Pavement	Subway	Underground
ce-box	Refrigerator	Trunk	Boot (of a car)

. *Answers will vary but children should add four more examples to the table.*

Challenger

1.

a) It gives me great pleasure …
b) Thanks mate. Don't mention …
c) I've got a splitting headache.
d) If it was me I'd go.
e) I can't get in, the door's locked.

2. *Answers will vary but children should watch some Australian TV programmes and make a list of words that we do not use.*

Language investigation 2

Check it out

(see Practice below)

Practice

1.

Latin or Greek	*Meaning*	*Two examples of words (These will vary)*
nova (Latin)	new	novel, novelty
photo (Greek)	light	photograph, photosynthesis
bi (Latin)	two	bicycle, bilingual
-ology (Greek)	a study of	sociology, theology
centum (Latin)	one hundred	century, centipede
bio (Greek)	life	biography, biology
micro (Greek)	small	microscope, microphone
audio (Latin)	sound	audible, auditory

2.

And the good wyfe answerde that she coude speke no frenshe. And the marchaunt was angry for he also coude speke no frenshe, but wold have hadde egges and she understode hym not. And thenne at laste a nother sayd that he wolde have eyren. Then the good wyf sayd that she understod hym wel.

a) *Answers will vary but children should underline the words they cannot understand.*

b) In a book about literature in the 15th century.

Challenger

1.

a) The passage is from a play because it is set out in a certain way.

b) to g) *Answers will vary*